CW01310871

MARCUS J YOUNG
STRATEGIES

Text and artwork copyright © 2020, Marcus J. Young
Edited by Marcus J. Young | Art Direction by Brett Thompson
Photography from Unsplash.com and used with permission.
All rights reserved. No portion of this book may be reproduced, stored in a retrieval system, or transmitted in any form or by any means, mechanical, electronic, photocopying, recording, or otherwise, without written permission from the publisher.

TABLE OF CONTENTS

	Introduction	4
	Foreword	6
1	Define Your Enemies	8
2	You too Have Been an Enemy	10
3	Choose an Enemy	12
4	Drowning in Enemies	16
5	A Humiliated Enemy	18
6	A Soaring Faith	20
7	Why Pray for Enemies? Part 1	22
8	Why Pray for Enemies? Part 2	24
9	Love Your Enemies Part 1	28
10	Love Your Enemies Part 2	30
11	Forgive Your Enemies	32
12	How to View an Enemy	34
13	To Judge or to Bless?	36
14	A Call to Bless Your Enemies	40
15	The Enemy – Imprisoned Anger	42

16	Kind Revenge	44
17	Overcome Evil with Good	46
18	Enemies are Treasure	48
19	How an Enemy Becomes Treasure	52
20	The Ministry of Reconciliation	54
21	Laugh at the Challenge	56
22	Was Jesus Ever Mean?	58
23	Don't Fear Your Enemy	60
24	Perfect for Enemies	64
25	Honor Your Enemies Part 1	66
26	Honor Your Enemies Part 2	68
27	Chase Your Enemies Part 1	70
28	Chase Your Enemies Part 2	72
29	Celebrate God with Your Enemies	76
30	Find Rest with Your Enemies	78
	Final Thoughts	80
	Gratitude & Acknowledgements	82

INTRODUCTION

Are there things about the church that make her feel glorious to you? If you looked at her through a stranger's eyes, would this church capture your imagination and awe, or would she offer only a faint shadow of spiritual attractiveness?

This booklet is a pathway into the depths of God's love beyond imagination—through loving enemies. Praying for, blessing and loving enemies is massively beneficial to us personally! If the church could embrace this lifestyle, it would become an expanding firework display of who God is, bursting like thousands of candle lights from a mountain in the darkness. Loving enemies is the glory of God beautifying his church, the depths of his intimate love.

It may be helpful to ask, "What is an enemy?" An enemy is, in simplest terms, an estranged son or daughter of our Father. We may not like them, they may be evil or unworthy, but God has declared enemies "good!" by the peace of his cross.

Engaging our enemies in love may be one of Jesus' most powerful strategies he offers for demonstrating God's kingdom. See Matthew 5 and Luke 6. This enemy love is the litmus test that we are true sons and daughters of a heavenly Papa. It is a lifestyle that perfectly and mercifully expresses his heart.

This booklet will guide you on a 30-day journey of loving both your personal enemies and the enemies of the church at large. It will open your eyes to the spiritual treasure buried in actively loving enemies and guide you in how to love your enemies the way Jesus did.

This booklet was written to help serve the countercultural justice movement. One that knows justice is demonstrated by sparking fires of love and mercy for perpetrators of evil all over the planet.

You may not finish this journey in exactly 30 days, but remain encouraged and committed to chase these 30 entries all the way to the beautiful finish line. It will give you a substantially freer place to live from and light up the skies with Jesus' fame.

FOREWORD

We traveled to a rebel army village on the side of a steep, forested mountain in Mindanao, Philippines. Military lookouts were hidden in the leafy canopy above us. Over a lunch of mountain rice and grilled chicken, I sat on the porch with the head commander of the Maoist rebel movement in the region.

The commander was a handsome woman, dressed in plain clothing suited to the area. She had a kind face. Perhaps the face of a mother? I wondered. I could also see the deep creases marking years of determination and struggle.

I glanced at her over a bite of chicken. "What do you think of prayer, Commander?"

She tilted her head back and looked hard at the ceiling, her lips a thin line. "I haven't prayed in 30 years."

"Can I have your permission to get some churches to pray for you?" I queried.

She looked at me with flat eyes. "The church will not pray for me. They don't like our New People's Army even a little."

A pain lanced through my heart at her words. Why do our Philippine churches have this reputation?

I persisted, "I could get 10 or so churches to pray for you. Can I have your permission? I would like to do this."

The commander offered a slight shrug and smiled. "It would take a miracle for the church to pray for me...but okay."

This woman grew up in the church and rejected it in her early 20's as providing any hope for her people. Her people have suffered injustice, mostly from the wealthy and the systems of monetary interest which keep them in servitude similar to the black sharecroppers of the rural south after the American Civil War.

Most of the global church sides with the greater Filipino population in feeling that when a Communist movement begins picking up arms, too many innocent people suffer. The very injustice that these rebels rise up to fight forms them into its own tools inflicting pain. War always has a negative impact on the local populous. Because of this suffering, rebel leaders become less human and more evil in our eyes. Often the church is scared of these leaders. Would Jesus be?

The commander went on to expose her heart and needs for prayer with me. This included prayers that her two sons would understand the many days and months she couldn't be home because of her service to the country as a Marxist. I left feeling deeply convicted to make sure she and all those others who are viewed as enemies of the church around the world know that we, God's people, love them.

I am accepting the challenge. Will you?

 # DEFINE YOUR ENEMIES

> *"My innocence is near. Who will go to judgment with me? Let us stand up together. Who is my enemy? Let him come near to me."*
>
> **Isaiah 50:8, The Aramaic Bible: The Isaiah Targum**

All of us have enemies, whether we are aware of it or not. These may be people who have deeply wounded us or hurt those we love. Often, they are people who have rejected us. Perhaps they threatened a certain part of our lives, something sacred to us or something essential to our wellbeing.

Think deeply on this. Does a name or face come to mind? Is it a challenging family member, a cutthroat competitor, your boss, a colleague, a former leader, a soldier, a terrorist or a political figure?

The Brilliance, a liturgical soft rock band, published a song that begins with the lyrics, **"When I look into the face of my enemy, I see my brother."** How do you see the face of your enemy?

Consider a time when your enemy hurt you. What did you feel about them then? Did you feel any bitterness, anger, sadness, rebellion, revenge or hatred toward them? And what about now, how do you feel about them at this moment?

How do you see this enemy? Jesus asks that we view our enemies as people already purchased by him and who are, or may one day be, brothers and sisters in Christ.

Reflective Actions

Let these prayers be meditative. Pause when you have a thought or a feeling rise up. Take a long moment to reflect on it and see if God leads you into a deeper prayer experience.

Prayer | "Spirit of Truth, fill me. Come into the hidden parts of my soul, into the nooks and crannies. Help me identify my enemies."

Ask Your Father | "Where is my pain? Who is the cause of this pain?"

Meditation | "Today I consider God is with me on this journey and even if I do not feel it, I forgive this enemy because God forgives my enemy."

Breakthrough | "I bring my feelings to you, Father; every wound that pains and every scar that constricts and knots. Even if I only feel pain and numbness, I choose to imagine your love like heavenly breaker waves sweeping over me, knocking down old walls. I open the door of my heart wide to this powerful love!"

YOU TOO HAVE BEEN AN ENEMY

> *"While we were still enemies, Christ reconciled us to the Father by his death."*
>
> *Romans 5:10[1]*

Remember where you came from as a newly born-again believer—you came out from enemy territory waving a white flag of surrender.

When Adam and Eve ate the fruit in the Garden of Eden, we sided with the serpent in his rebellion against our Creator. We tried to make a small theft of a huge thing: the Creator's Spirit of Wisdom to judge good and evil, to divide, to judge between things as he did in creation...dividing light from darkness, times and seasons, the earth and the waters, woman from man, rest and work. But judgement is God's work. This includes judging good people and evil enemies.

Through the ages we have plundered the earth's resources instead of stewarding them as a good gift that speaks daily of God like an expressive book or a beautiful painting. We have shed rivers of innocent blood into her soil building our inspiring monuments and magnificent empires—blood that speaks of a spotless Lamb's cost to redeem his created world. We, the caretakers of planet earth, have taken lives that reflect the Imago Dei, God's image.

Humanity is a race of enemies. Without the mercy of the cross, our good becomes evil and our evil works change for good, and we create a tangle of God's good creation[2]. We cannot consistently live to our aspirations, even the best and kindest of us.

But Jesus cherished me, even when I was his enemy and he is the way back to the good Father that every heart longs for. He is my good. I may fail many times over, but God has a grand purpose in Jesus that supersedes all injustice in the world today and forever. Come, Lord Jesus!

Reflective Actions

Prayer | "Jesus, kill my incriminating nature. Resurrect my heart to receive your Love. Thank you."

Ask Your Father | "What did I have in common with my enemy before I was reconciled to you? Show me who I am now that I am in you! Doesn't your love always pursue me? Aren't you a true father who always runs to his child?"

Meditation | "For since our friendship with God was restored by the death of his Son while we were still his enemies, we will certainly be saved through the life of his Son" (Romans 5:10, NLT). Put this in your own words and ponder it throughout the day.

Breakthrough | "I am hidden in you, the Christ Himself. I am freed from any slavery to the domain of sin. I am unbound from death, unshackled from sin. I am no longer your enemy. Wonder of wonders! The enormity of this gift! I can worship with abandon. So, I come now with a bold and carefree child's heart to a great throne bubbling over with grace and kindness where my Papa sits with open arms."

---

[1] Translation by Marcus Young

[2] For example, often our choices to serve, give and love enable dependencies in others. Consequentially, present evil can become good because what some people in one generation win by exploitation, others in a subsequent generation may use for charity.

CHOOSE AN ENEMY

"At that time Jesus went up a hill to pray and spent the whole night there praying to God. When day came, he called his disciples to him and chose twelve of them, whom he named apostles: Simon (whom he named Peter) and his brother Andrew; James and John, Philip and Bartholomew, Matthew and Thomas, James son of Alphaeus, and Simon (who was called the Patriot), Judas son of James, and Judas Iscariot, who became the traitor."

Luke 6:12-16, The Good News Translation

If you don't feel you have an enemy, you need one; not an enemy to hate, but one to love.

This may be difficult to believe. However, Jesus prayed all night before choosing his inner circle of 12 men and one of his chosen few was his enemy, the one who would betray him. As you venture out with us on this amazing journey of praying for enemies, you too will see the wonders to be discovered by loving enemies.

Jesus' example was to choose a traitor to mentor—his personal traitor. This enemy didn't learn from him very well. This traitor even set him up for betrayal and a Roman criminal's cross. Why was this enemy so necessary for our Messiah? Is this a model teaching us not to fear our enemies, even those in our own close circle? Maybe it is even a model for us to work with our enemies and give them a chance, even if the forecast doesn't look redemptive.

Reflective Actions

Prayer | "Father, it is my desire to love like you love. I ask that you remove my blinders and clear my eyes so that I can see my enemies, who they are and who they are destined to be. I confess my need for your help to pray for these traitors—my enemies. It's difficult for me, God, so difficult. Help me with the pain."

Ask Your Father | "Who are the enemies of my calling and my internal peace?" Speak their names before God. "What did my enemies do to me or to those I love?" God knows your thoughts intimately, but honesty about all your feelings in prayer brings them undeniably into his healing presence.

Meditation | Following Jesus' example is not just important, it is critical. Why? He is our highest example of knowing and experiencing the Father abundantly. If you are still struggling with forgiveness, it's okay. Keep speaking your desire to forgive your enemy every day as you read this guide. The miracle will come.

Breakthrough | All of heaven is backing you on this daily journey. Do you know that God has great hope for your heart to expand its capacity to live in his love?

"Papa God, I receive the grace of your Spirit and the washing of your Word. I release _____ and speak forgiveness over them. I accept that the Father loves them right now and that Jesus died for them too."

"Keep speaking your desire to forgive your enemy every day..."

DROWNING IN ENEMIES

"All day long I feel humiliated and am overwhelmed with shame, before the vindictive enemy who ridicules and insults me."

Psalms 44:15-16, NET Bible

Maybe you feel this enemy experiment isn't going very well? For one thing, you simply don't have time to deal with enemies. For another, you may feel the shame of failure because your emotional capacity when dealing with certain enemies is too limited. It seems best to stay numb and keep moving.

At surface value, it appears Jesus made a big mistake when he chose a betrayer to be part of his core team...and for only 30 pieces of silver. Jesus could have found that in a fish! It was a devastating mistake. His leaders in training all scattered. He was captured by jealous and outraged religious leaders.

I hope you can see a different kingdom at work here. We don't know why Judas Iscariot was disappointed in Jesus' leadership. Was it the hope of riches that he hung on Jesus' rise to power? Did Judas finally see that Jesus didn't have that kind of political ambition? Jesus viewed life from a different perspective, just like you can.

At the last supper, after Judas took the morsel Jesus offered, Satan entered into him. Jesus said to him, "What you are going to do, do quickly" (John 13:27[3]). *This is one of the clearest pictures we have that enemies can be a direct tool of the chief enemy, Satan. But even when Satan moves, there is a greater purpose at work, a God-sized purpose. It was this purpose in God that Jesus was submitted to. All the while tasting, sensing and looking towards the Joy of his Father's love.*

"Jesus, who for the joy that was set before him endured the cross, despising the shame, and is seated at the right hand of the throne of God" (Hebrews 12:2). Like Jesus when he faced the cross, you also are here with a God-sized purpose...a purpose even at work when enemies rage like they did at Jesus. Those moments are often your most important ones.

Reflective Actions

Prayer | "God, show me the bigger purpose and give me meaningful hope so that I am not drowning in the cruelty of my enemies. I don't want to die of bitterness of soul so protect me from harboring offense. Make your love and grace a refuge for my heart as I learn to love my enemies."

Ask Your Father | God is love. His purposes will follow love. "What is your purpose for me?"

Listen and write down what he says. Allow his torrent of joy to soak deep into your soul!

Meditation | Truth: Even my enemies must serve the glory of God's good purposes in me today.

Breakthrough | "Let the Niagara Falls of Heaven's will crash down into me. I open myself wide to you. I see now that what Satan uses to kill and steal and destroy, you can use to bring reconciliation, eternal life and glory!"

---

[3] Unless otherwise noted, all Bible verses are from the English Standard Version (ESV)

day 5 — A HUMILIATED ENEMY

"Rather you have saved us from our enemies, and have humiliated those who hate us."

Psalms 44:7, ESV Translation

How does God save us from our enemies? He calls them his friends. *Really?!* Yes, he reconciled them to their heavenly Father (who is also our Father). But how can naming them "friend" magically turn them into friends? It's true, they may still hate God and hate his church. However, if Jesus has reconciled them, now it is our work as the church to declare the good news of reconciliation to them. Loving enemies is a work of the Holy Spirit. It is activated in faith. We look beyond the temporary facts of someone's sin and broken choices to the eternal truth and grace of God's work in Jesus.

How does an enemy get humiliated (Psalms 44:7)? It's simple really; it comes from the amazing love of Jesus that radiates from you when you are hated, abused and ill-treated. For a hater, this is humiliation, about as easy to swallow as a handful of vitamins and only a teaspoon of water! But for a lover, persecution can plunge us into joyful abandonment to God and intimate friendship with him.

Your love for your enemies is confrontational. It is a great, offensive weapon. How did God humiliate the Jews? He sent Jesus as a babe into the virgin womb, causing a religious scandal. Jesus entered the fray not as a political Messiah but as a spiritual rabbi to confront Rome with his Father's heart. Frankly, it offends most of the world that a Creator would name us enemies and then become a creature who could die for love of his enemies to remake us into friends and family. Love confronts. Love calls us to something higher, something God-like. That is why we need the Holy Spirit to help us live on this heavenly plane.

Reflective Actions

Prayer | "God, help me bless my enemy. Help me to love them, to see them as you see them, and to bless them to walk in their destiny as a child of God! Reveal the places inside of me that are still a home to bitterness towards others." Finding this hard? "Help me, God" prayers are always okay here.

Ask Your Father | If you need to, take a few minutes to let your heart move into worship. Listen to a song. Get quiet.

"Am I still holding any bitterness towards my enemy?"

"Do I feel as though it is impossible to truly and fully forgive them?"

"What is one thing I can do today to actively show love to my enemy?"

Meditation | As you follow what Holy Spirit[4] showed you to do to actively love your enemy, be thoughtful and learn. Action brings more understanding. Have your actions shifted anything in your own perspective about enemies? If they have, jot those down—don't lose the moment!

Breakthrough | "I choose today to partner with your Spirit and purposes, even if I don't feel it. I believe that as I meditate on who you are and confess your truth that I will be transformed by the renewing of my mind! So, Father, I forgive _____." Take whatever the Holy Spirit says and make it a priority to do it today or tomorrow.

---

[4] Holy Spirit is a person of the Godhead, therefore, in this book, we often remove "the" from "the Holy Spirit."

Love Your Enemy

A SOARING FAITH

"But to you who are willing to listen, I say, love your enemies! Do good to those who hate you. Bless those who curse you. Pray for those who hurt you."

Luke 6:27-28, New Living Translation

Do we have faith to hear what Jesus said? According to Romans 5:10[5] we were enemies ourselves, but by Jesus' cross every enemy, all of us, were reconciled even before we said yes. Now even our own enemy stands in that same accepted position before the Father. All that remains is their choice to follow the way of Jesus. So now, we need to pray for their salvation by His life. By salvation, we mean that the universal kingdom rule of God would collide with their little kingdom—their family and friends, their wealth, favor, influence—and that in every way, the purposes of heaven, the designs of heaven, would inundate even the cracks and crevices of their world like flood waters.

Loving all our enemies is a supernatural work. That is why it is first a work of the cross. Only the cross is powerful enough to break strongholds of hatred. Jesus modeled love on his cross by forgiving us as his enemies and by giving us a direct connection to heaven and our Papa God once again.

Do we believe in a God that is powerful enough and good enough to save the most vile of people? Is our faith in that kind of God strong? We are on a journey of loving enemies, and we need faith to believe that God can truly redeem anyone we consider vile and harmful.

Reflective Actions

Prayer | Let's ask for a big faith to believe in a God who is happy to redeem anyone: "Jesus, increase my faith in your goodness, a goodness that can and will overtake even my enemies. May reconciliation fill the church like praise songs! Align us to Heaven's heart! Conform us to the forgiveness of the cross. Give us courage to know you in the invigorating challenge of loving enemies. Father, use this alignment to your heart and our declarative prayers as your people to unleash resurrection life into our enemies' lives. Cascade expressions of beautiful salvation all around them!"

Ask Your Father | Consider the example of Paul the Apostle. He wept when he spoke of enemies in the third chapter of his letter to the Philippians.

"When I speak of my enemies, can I cry for them?"

"How can I experience the same compassion that your Son did regarding Jerusalem's leaders killing his prophets in Luke 13? 'How often I wanted to gather your children together, just as a hen gathers her brood under her wings, and you would not have it!' (NASB)"

Quiet your soul. Allow Holy Spirit to minister to you and reveal how he feels regarding enemies. Record what he says.

Meditation | God embraced me while I was still an enemy and wants to do the same for those around me.

Breakthrough | "Oh, Father! Break my heart for my enemies!" (You can name them here too.) "Help me weep the tears of your heart and comprehend the radical mercies of a God who embraced me while I was still an enemy!"

---

[5] For if, while we were enemies, we were reconciled to God through the death of his Son, by much more, having been reconciled, we will be saved through his life. (Romans 5:10 LEB)

WHY PRAY FOR ENEMIES?
PART 1

"Then my enemies will retreat, turning back in the day when I pray."

Psalms 56:10, The Aramaic Bible

In the Kingdom of God, we operate very differently than what makes sense to the world. This can be called a "paradox." A paradox operates counterintuitively to how we naturally logic something out. Jesus may ask us to do things that are not the norm, but it causes us to operate in spiritual strength rather than our natural abilities. This is especially true in praying for our enemies.

The Holy Spirit empowers us when we choose to pray for our enemies. Take Paul's famous words for example, "when I am weak, then I am strong" (2 Corinthians 12:10). How does this paradox make sense? When we allow God to work in our lives rather than us taking control, he is able to display HIS mighty glory through us and enable us to do and be things we cannot in our weakness.

Paradox is a powerful implement for rapidly deconstructing spiritual strongholds. This holds true both in our personal lives and also in spheres of influence. This counterintuitive truth forces us into a divine exchange. This exchange will confront darkness and bring light in the blink of an eye. We can think of this exchange as a paradigm shift that can broadly impact our mind, will, emotions and spirit.

Because the wounds received from our enemies evoke powerful emotion for us as individuals, the paradox of loving and praying for someone who we perceive did something hateful is often one of the most paradigm-shifting encounters with his heart that Jesus offers us as his followers.

Reflective Actions

Prayer | "Father, today I choose to depend on your strength and not on my own. I choose your love and your peace that is beyond my comprehension. I lay down my shield and my weapons used in warfare against my human enemy. You are my protection, my shield and my hope! Yet again, I release any negative or bitter thoughts and emotions towards my enemy to you. Wash me clean like a mountain spring! I trust you to fight on my behalf. With you I fear no evil. With you, I am safe."

Ask Your Father | Can you see how small an enemy's meanness is from God's perspective, like dust mites in the wind?

"How else do you see enemies, Papa God? What is your heart for them?"

Meditation | Putting down my weapons allows God to be my protector and deliverer. "I lean not on my own understanding, love not from my own love. Where I am weak, God's strength is perfected in me. I can love my enemy because God's love in me is perfect!"

Breakthrough | "Holy Spirit, bless my enemy today! Bless their health, their minds, their thoughts, their emotions, their joy, and their hopes. Help them to somehow touch you in prayer. Help them to find you, the amazing One. Bless those they love too: their families, their friends, their companions. Have mercy on them, Jesus."

WHY PRAY FOR ENEMIES?
PART 2

"If you love only those who love you, what reward is there for that? Even corrupt tax collectors do that much. If you are kind only to your friends, how are you different from anyone else? Even pagans do that."

Matthew 5:46-47, New Living Translation

When we begin to pray for our enemies in line with Jesus' command, "pray for those who abuse you,"[6] it is helpful to understand this prayer is for our benefit. It is more than a request for our enemies to change. God only commands us to do things because of the blessing attached for his children. He isn't giving us busy work or chores that he is too busy to do. A command is a blessing for us because God is entirely good and therefore intentionally good in his actions and words.

He commands the blessing in Psalms 133:3[7] not only because the church that unifies in prayer and heart can be blessed but because *every command* invokes a blessing of heaven for us when we accept it! When we obey by unifying, God commands the blessing attached to that obedient unity and the blessing pours into our lives!

Obeying Jesus' words to "love and pray for your enemies" is also a strategic, counterintuitive activity that forces us to live by the Spirit of Love, Power, and a Sound Mind[8] and not of our own capacity. In loving our enemies, we receive a great multitude of blessings, and we vivify—bring out the beauty of—the good news of God's kingdom.

Reflective Actions

Prayer | "Father, I let go of bitterness toward my enemies. I open up my negative feelings that hinder blessings from you, Papa God. Do a new work in me, even if it is one I may not yet understand. I choose to forgive, pray for and love my enemies so I can experience your glorious freedom!"

Ask Your Father | "How can I show a little love for my enemy today?"

"Reveal to me and my community the blessings attached to loving and praying for enemies."

Meditation | Meditate on what you hear the Father say and write down at least 5 of these blessings that you will claim, accept and rest in.

Practice choosing love today. When I choose to love my enemy even a little, anger begins to fall away, hatred dries up, and sadness dissipates. God is able to begin to give me His perspective of them.

Breakthrough | How vast your goodness is, God! Thank you for desiring good things for us! Thank you for your blessings and total freedom from bondage to bitterness and hate!

Since I am blessed when I obey God's commands, I will trust that he will honor and pour out blessing on my decision to pray for and love my enemies.

---

[6] Luke 6:27

[7] Behold, how good and pleasant it is when brothers dwell in unity! It is like the precious oil on the head, running down on the beard, on the beard of Aaron, running down on the collar of his robes! It is like the dew of Hermon, which falls on the mountains of Zion! For there the Lord has commanded the blessing, life forevermore. (Ps 133:1-3)

[8] 2 Timothy 1:7

# LOVE YOUR ENEMIES
PART 1

"Blessed are the peacemakers, for they shall be called sons of God."

Matthew 5:9, ESV Translation

Did you know that people recognize us as sons and daughters of God by our love for our enemies? We can call this "proof of life"—something that shows the Holy Spirit really has activated our spiritual DNA.

This heart of peace makes us different from the world, and it shows others that we have something unique and special inside of us. We may be judged unfairly as Christ followers, but we are also affording people a true and beautiful look at God when they see this heart of peace in us.

It may be helpful to ask, "What is an enemy?" An enemy is simply an estranged son or daughter of our Father. We may not like them, and they may be evil, but God has declared enemies "good!" by the peace of his cross. They are reborn, a new creation before him...if they so choose to accept the new spiritual world order. This is why the gospel is GOOD NEWS!

This new reality can be said of deceitful, self-serving politicians, murderers, brothel keepers or whatever "lowlife" you might choose. In the words of Oswald Chambers, "Men are not *going* to be redeemed; they *are* redeemed"[9] In the words of Jesus, "It is finished!"[10] In the words of Paul, "In Christ, God was reconciling the world to himself, not counting their trespasses against them, and entrusting to us the message of reconciliation."[11] People still have the free choice of saying no to this great redemption but it is the job of the church, your work and our work, to treat humanity according to the new order—the redemption of the world.

Reflective Actions

Prayer | "Help me, Father God, to see people as saved and going to heaven before I judge them as lost and going to hell. You came to seek and to save. Give me faith for them and courage to prophetically proclaim your goodness into their lives! Make me bold in your goodness, my dear Papa."

Ask Your Father | "I pause in your presence to sense and to see, who I am as your son or daughter with full family status."

Meditation | There is a great rest in knowing God's love. There is a great peace in laying down our weapons and loving through our access to every spiritual blessing and all authority in heaven and on earth. I choose to use this access and authority to love my enemy, to be a minister of reconciliation instead of hate.

Breakthrough | I have access to the entire inheritance of the heavenly realm. This begins with the never-ending love of the Father and his provision for everything I need for abundance of life and living his purposes now! I can be at peace in this and carry this peace with me anywhere I go.

"I breathe you in, better than the air I breathe. I breathe you out into the world around me, radiant love I can rest my heart in! Your kingdom of peace goes with me on this journey of loving my enemy."

---

[9] Chambers, O. (1996). *Conformed to His Image*. London: Marshall, Morgan & Scott.

[10] John 19:30

[11] 2 Corinthians 5:19

LOVE YOUR ENEMIES
PART 2

"You have heard that it was said, 'You shall love your neighbor and hate your enemy.' But I say to you, 'Love your enemies and pray for those who persecute you, so that you may be sons of your Father who is in heaven.'"

Matthew 5:43-44, ESV Translation

"So that you may be..." Being a son is a formative process. We may have said a big YES to Jesus as Lord, but now we need a daily YES to be conformed to his glory as spiritual sons and daughters.

We have full family status as children of unmerited favor—grace. When we accept God's grace and extend this same grace to others, we look more like the sons and daughters of God that we were redeemed to be.

Enemies can be thought of as "grace-growers,"[12] people who challenge us. They are people that we may not like—our hecklers. They are our opportunity to choose to extend grace and thereby grow spiritually, especially in spiritual fruit. They could be the people we most need. Their criticisms and persecution help chisel off our rough edges and unveil the masterpiece of who we are meant to be.

Why is it useful to mature in the fruit of the Spirit? When spiritual fruit is ripe in our lives, this means we are seed-bearers. Wherever we go, kingdom seeds get planted, even in the hardest kinds of places.

Spiritual fruit impacts the atmosphere; love, joy, peace, patience, kindness, goodness, faithfulness, gentleness and self-control (Galatians 5:22-23) are the values of a kingdom culture, and carry different undercurrents that shape culture.

Spiritual fruit that is not tainted by spiritual pride or legalism (rules) is a stunning fare to be shared with a starving world.

Reflective Actions

Prayer | "Jesus, train my heart to abide in your heart. You are the Vine-keeper, the Gardener of my heart—I swing open wide the gate of my heart so you can do what you do best and make me like you."

Ask Your Father | Take a deep breath, and slowly let it out. Listen to your Papa's heart. Enemies can be the greatest "grace-growers" because they give us the most opportunities to grow in grace of spiritual fruit.

"What life-giving fruits do I need to grow in?"

"How are my current enemies growing grace in my life?"

Meditation | "I am a seed-bearer, a tree full of ripe fruit. I am a life-giving tree like You—my enemies find a fruit-feast of Jesus' love when they are sitting in my shade."

Breakthrough | "Father, show your heart through my heart to enemies everywhere. Increase my grace in growing the fruit of _____ , so that my enemy, _____ , will encounter your glory—the stunning beauty of your character. Overwhelm their hearts with your love and turn their gaze to you."

---

[12] As taught by popular speaker, Graham Cooke.

FORGIVE YOUR ENEMIES

"Jesus said to [the apostles] again, 'Peace be with you. As the Father has sent me, even so I am sending you.' And when he had said this, he breathed on them and said to them, 'Receive the Holy Spirit. If you forgive the sins of any, they are forgiven them; if you withhold forgiveness from any, it is withheld.'"

John 20:21-23, ESV Translation

These words above were for Jesus' apostles. This is a big moment—the first time Jesus offers the Holy Spirit freely to his people. It is a post-resurrection moment, a new creation impartation akin to when he breathed life into the clay of man that he had formed.

Jesus breathes the Holy Spirit into his young leaders, commissioning them. With this new creation moment, he gives them a flexible job description: "To forgive or not to forgive." It isn't a command. This is a descriptor of the power they were given. It is a statement built on what had just happened on the cross. *To not forgive is to resist the amazing gift God gave us in having the power and ability to rely on the Holy Spirit to forgive.*

Look at Jesus: He forgave the world while they hated him and were dead in sin. He died for the very people who spat on him, nailed him to a cross, and brutally murdered him. Following the resurrection Jesus even forgave Peter, who denied him three times. He forgave this dear friend and key leader who had completely turned his back against him. He then gave Peter great hope, indicating that one day Peter would have the strength to actually die as his Lord did.

Jesus modeled this and then imparted it. *"Whose sins you forgive"* is the mission statement of the church. It is our fantastic news of reconciliation to the Father, now spoken to others by us, through the breath of the Holy Spirit.

Reflective Actions

Prayer | "Jesus, give me grace to see my enemies with different eyes. Help me to stop looking at my enemies as sinners going to hell, but rather open my eyes to see them the way you do: 100% forgiven people that your Spirit is wooing to be your own mighty heroes to demonstrate righteousness and justice on the planet."

Ask Your Father | "Papa, show me how you see my enemy. Father, I want to forgive powerfully like you do, so show me how you forgave me and how you have forgiven my enemy."

Meditation | I can choose to not forgive an enemy, but this is the antithesis of who I am, of what the peace of the cross is. If Jesus empowers me with the Holy Spirit to forgive, if he died to forgive, if he rose to forgive, how can I not rely on the Holy Spirit to provide me the grace to forgive?

Breakthrough | Forgiveness prayer is a daily action. Don't feel it? You should still pray it. Be comforted in God's love today and then from that place pray, love, and forgive those who create evil in our world. "Holy Spirit: I believe! I choose your forgiveness, for me and for my enemy. I choose the cross, I choose grace, I choose freedom and healing. I forgive _____."

HOW TO VIEW AN ENEMY

"Whatever is true, whatever is honorable, whatever is just, whatever is pure, whatever is lovely, whatever is commendable, if there is any excellence, if there is anything worthy of praise, think about these things."

Philippians 4:8, ESV Translation

How we view enemies determines the size of our family.[13]

Paul marvels in his second letter to the Corinthians, "we have concluded this: that one has died for all, therefore all have died." And because of this, "from now on, we regard no one according to the flesh"[14]. By "flesh," Paul means the viewpoint of fallen man. "We are now called to esteem all people as newly made in Christ imploring them to accept the acceptance of God by their own free choice."[15] God's forgiveness by the cross is unconditional, our acceptance of it is carte blanche.

God will not force his love because, when forced, love becomes fragile and breaks. It is irrevocably a love already freely given. Therefore, my love is not meant to be hoarded by me until a sinner repents but given in overflow until he/she sees the beauty of Jesus. Enemies are my greatest opportunity to demonstrate this torrent of reconciling forgiveness so that the "kindness and forbearance and patience"[16] of God may lead them to repentance.

Reflective Actions

Prayer | "I pray not only for the eternal life of my enemies but for their alignment to the Kingdom of God. I pray for their families to see your blessings, and that your will would be done in their lives."

Ask Your Father | "Is there any healing from any pain caused by betrayals and abuse I need to receive? Anything you wish to speak to me about my own healing from the meditation on Philippians 4:8?"

Meditation | Read Philippians 4:8 again. Use this as your lens to see enemies and pray for them. This will help us sift and hone our prayers into heavenly weapons of goodness and kindness. Eight steps to sift out a potent prayer for your enemy:

True: Begin with truth, however brutal and emotional.

Honorable: Wrestle out ways to give honor with that truth.

Just: Seek out restorative justice through reconciliatory prayers and actions.

Pure: Practice purity of heart by encountering God through enemies in even the smallest glimmers.

Lovely: See gracious Abba's gaze of love on your enemy.

Commendable: Is it a prayer you would find admirable if prayed for you?

Excellent: Is there a high bar in these thoughts and prayers?

Praiseworthy: Would this prayer feel like praise of your enemy, praise of God's heart and ways?

Breakthrough | The pure in heart see God... I can see the Prince of Peace at work in my enemies today, on their behalf and on mine. I can see God healing my own heart and giving great freedom here!

---

[13] Consider Matthew 18:15, "'If he listens to you, you have won your brother.' It doesn't say you have won the argument, but that you have won a brother." — Joel Hill

[14] 2 Corinthians 5:14b,16a

[15] 2 Corinthians 5:17a, 20b — Paraphrase

[16] Romans 2:4

TO JUDGE OR TO BLESS?

"Do not repay evil for evil or reviling for reviling, but on the contrary, bless, for to this you were called, that you may obtain a blessing."

1 Peter 3:9, ESV Translation

This is a climactic point in Peter's letter—we are called to be a blessing. Our primal DNA of blessing traces back to the Abrahamic promise.

When suffering comes from others Peter responds, "It's time for judgement to begin at the house of God."[17] Being judged is a sensitive issue for us because in our minds it indicates we are wrong or makes us think of punishment. This is not a problem we can solve or even clarify in a short meditation but here are some useful ideas to bring before Holy Spirit to ask for further enlightenment.

» The love of the cross contains the full revelation of God's judgment and is the framework for understanding any judgment of God.

» Judgement was dispensed when wickedness had ripened, and Satan, the demonically infused principalities, and fallen people killed Jesus. God did not kill Jesus but neither did he protect him.

» Judgment is meant to bring redemptive blessing because the cross is reconciliatory in nature.

» When the church is judged by her enemies, she is judged as Jesus was; God allows it, but he does not personally strike her.

» The outcome of us submitting to this discipline should be blessing, hope and even salvation for our enemies.

» When we pass through cruciform discipline, the wonderful Spirit of glory rests on us,[18] and empowers us to speak authentic blessing.

> If judgement does really begin with us and we display rotten or pessimistic attitudes to those who make our lives miserable, how will that impact our enemies' ability to see Jesus' heart?[19]

Judgement must begin with the church so she can model the supernatural mercy and hope found in Jesus. There is emotional and spiritual sifting that comes as hardship at the hand of an enemy. Our joyful response to this sifting is a beacon of truth that can penetrate the demonic lies our enemies live under. *Bless unkind and evil people into the gift of the kingdom, don't curse them into hell.*

Reflective Actions

Prayer | "Jesus, uncover joy in my life, especially in these areas of pain. Help me to bless where I have previously cursed my enemy."

Ask Your Father | "Show me where my heart still struggles to bless those who have wounded me. How can I turn judgement into radical love opportunities and wounds into doors to blessing and grace?"

Meditation | In the spirit of your Philippians 4:8 meditation, look for themes that God had you pray. From these themes, if you haven't already, write out a blessing for your enemies. Begin to pray those blessings as declarations every day.

Breakthrough | "Father, I believe (in Jesus) I am like YOU! By blessing in the face of judgement, I show the world my true DNA. I declare blessing on _____ today—encounter them with your grace Gospel!"

---

[17] 1 Peter 4:17

[18] 1 Peter 4:14

[19] Through love and service of our enemies, we can be a support to them as they go through the discipline of the Lord and it actually CAN have a restorative result. — Bill Johnson

"One of the best ways to strengthen a pure heart is by showing honor."

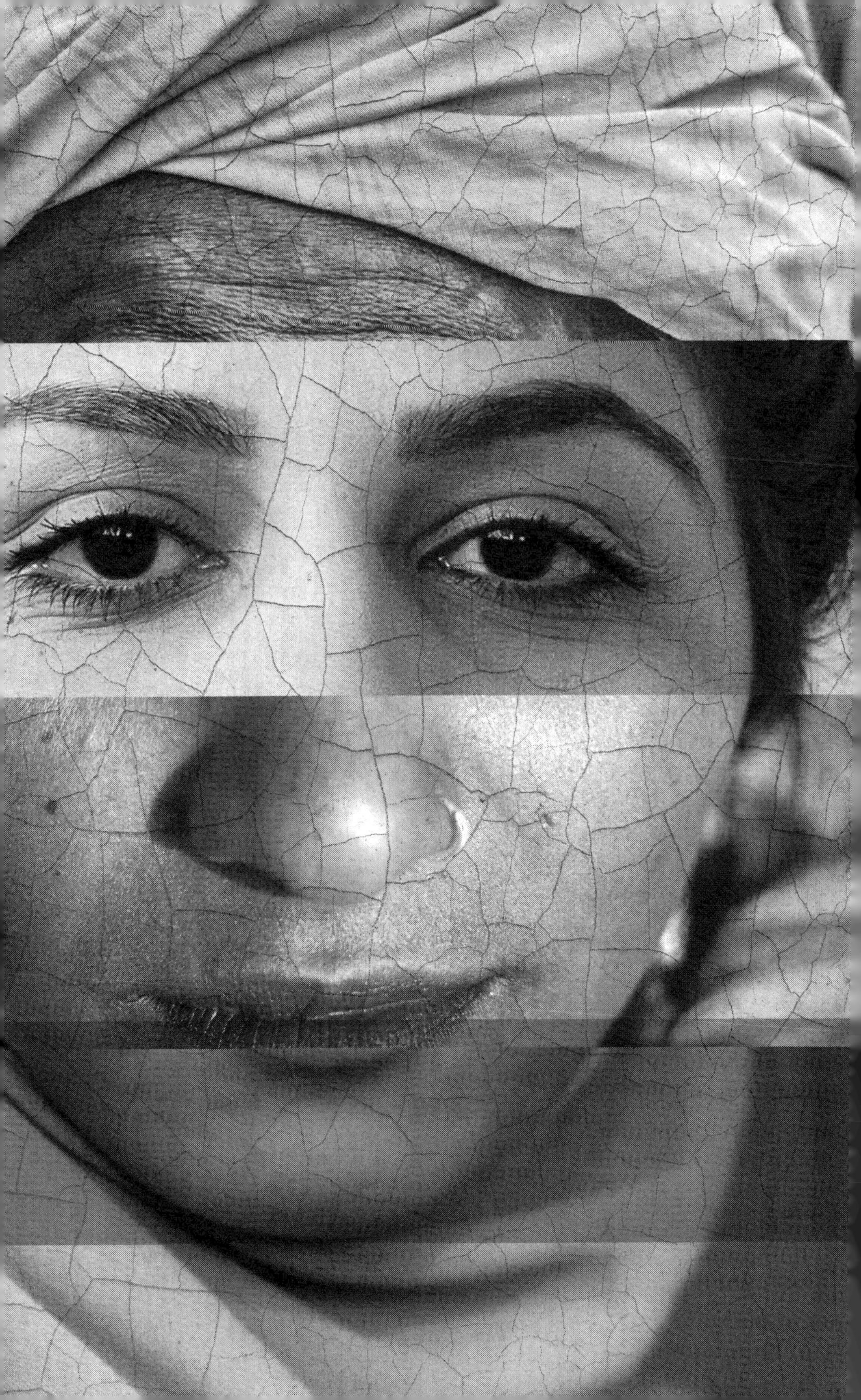

day 14 — A CALL TO BLESS YOUR ENEMIES

"Judge not, and you will not be judged; condemn not, and you will not be condemned; forgive, and you will be forgiven; give, and it will be given to you. Good measure, pressed down, shaken together, running over, will be put into your lap. For with the measure you use it will be measured back to you."

Luke 6:37–38, ESV Translation

First, let's put the lens of blessing on this passage. Do we want an increase of blessings in our lives? Then bless more. Speak with hope-filled kindness that thrusts people into the presence of God.

Is it more powerful to bless or to curse? Did God create the world in blessing or in cursing? *Could we believe today that blessing our enemy is a more powerful weapon for useful change than thinking negative thoughts or saying unkind words about them?*

Now let's put the eyeglasses of judgement on this passage. Matthew 7:2 does this clearly by saying, "by the standard that we judge others, we will be measured."[20] The scales of actual and personal judgement are set by us. This could possibly even refer to how we are eternally judged. Knowing that we set the rules of our own judgement should be a strong motivation for how kindly we treat our enemies.

Reflective Actions

Prayer | "Teach me to find beauty and joy that is at a higher heavenly reality than where I am experiencing pain. Train my lips to bless (even my enemies) from that place of high joy and beauty!"

Ask Your Father | "What is one way I can change a negative thought, emotion or word about my enemy into a blessing for them?"

Meditation | Imagine a town or city where only blessings and kind words of faith for others' lives were spoken. What would a place like that look like? What would be positive impacts on the health, happiness and prosperity of that city? Would others want to visit that city and learn from it?

Is there a parallel to this heavenly city? "And the city has no need of the sun nor of the moon to illuminate it, for the glory of God illuminated it, and its lamp is the Lamb. And the nations shall walk by means of its light. And the kings of the earth bring their glory into it" (Rev. 21:23-24 WUESTNT).

Continue to repeat the prayers for your enemies that you wrote down in the previous chapter. But this time, add powerful prayers of blessing, following the Philippians 4:8 guidelines.

Breakthrough | "As your child I am blessed, no matter what so I know I can bless from what I have—all of you, Jesus! From the foundation of my divine call I bless, it is a privilege to face judgment because I am so loved by my Papa. In his love there is so much freedom!"

[20] Paraphrase

day 15

THE ENEMY - IMPRISONED ANGER

"You heard that it was said by those of a previous time, 'You shall not commit murder, and whoever commits murder shall be subject to the judgment.' But, as for myself, I am saying to you that everyone who is provoked to anger against his brother shall be subject to the judgment."

Matthew 5:21-22, Wuest's Translation

You've heard the axiom, "we are often our own worst enemy." There is some truth in this as we are free to make self-devastating choices. However, Satan the Accuser is our worst enemy—not ourselves. Satan accused God and caused Eve to doubt. 1 John 3:8 calls sin "the works of the devil" as he is the progenitor of sin. Satan is an enemy God says is in his realm of wisdom to judge, not ours (see Jude 9).

But even if we accept Satan is the greatest enemy—not us—we still can be dangerous opponents of our own good if we listen to him. Especially when we say "No!" to God's Spirit and bear our own fruit. Like when we nurture anger toward someone, as Jesus equates harboring anger with murder.

Jesus goes on to say that if this anger begins to impact our speech in negative ways this makes us fit company for hell. Hello? It's so serious he recommends that even if you are doing something important, drop it now, run and get reconciled with the person you are offended at. Harboring personal anger is devastating because it judges us here and now, locking our hearts away from freedom, from full Presence of joy.

When Jesus saw the local children were being scolded and kept at arm's length by his leaders, he was indignant![21] It is not wrong to be angry about injustice on behalf of others but it's wrong to internalize and personalize that anger, letting it become a long standing sour attitude. Let your heart live from a higher plane where the power of God can infuse it. Our source is love, not anger. *According to the scriptures, anger and judgement are quick, short-term verbs. Love and mercy are constant, long-term verbs. Use Satan's strategy to anchor us in anger at our enemies to instead catch a heavenly updraft of forgiveness and joy.*

Reflective Actions

Prayer | "Jesus, I choose you. I say yes. I will not be a prisoner to anger by harboring it in my heart against anyone. I recognize that harboring anger anchors me to my pain and causes me to become bitter. And I want freedom!"

Ask Your Father | "Is there anyone that I am holding anger or jealousy against in my heart, big or small? What half-truth has Satan fed my mind to degrade their beauty as a person? I confess this to you, Papa."

Meditation | Read Matthew 5:21-26, reflecting on how easy it is to move from righteous anger to harboring judgmental anger and how wonderful it is to be spiraling in an updraft of God's mercy and forgiveness.

Breakthrough | "Today I release my anger and forgive _____ for _____." This person can even be a government, a leader... a manager or a mass shooter; it doesn't have to be someone you know personally. Find at least 2 things you can be thankful for about this person. Maybe even write them a kind note or schedule a coffee with them.

[21] Mark 10:14

day 16   KIND REVENGE

> *"Beloved, never avenge yourselves, but leave it to the wrath of God, for it is written, 'Vengeance is mine, I will repay, says the Lord.' To the contrary, 'if your enemy is hungry, feed him; if he is thirsty, give him something to drink; for by so doing you will heap burning coals on his head.'"*
>
> *Romans 12:19-20, ESV Translation*

Father or Saint Ambrose was a 4th century Bishop of Milan and an eloquent teacher in the church. He also was the early mentor of St. Augustine, who has had incredible formational impact on the church's theology. Ambrose recommends, "Since God said in the Old Testament, 'Vengeance is mine, I shall repay,' he says in the Gospel that we should pray for those who harm us in order that he who promised vengeance might not seek revenge against them. *For [God] wants to forgive by your will, which is fitting according to his promise.* But if you seek revenge, you have it, since the unjust man is punished more by his thoughts than by judicial severity."[22]

"God wants to forgive by our will." In like manner, Jesus commissioned his apostles by the Holy Spirit that "if you forgive the sins of any, they are forgiven, if you withhold forgiveness from any, it is withheld (John 20:23, ESV)."

Another ancient author reflects, *"If then you are benevolent to an enemy, you have rather spared yourself than him. And if you do him a kindness, you benefit yourself more than him."*[23] These aren't new ideas to the Church. They stem directly from Jesus' teachings. Are we willing to test them out and see if "the shoe fits" the Christian story?

Can we trust Jesus, the only worthy one to judge? He is the sacrificial Lamb of God and the only one worthy in heaven and on earth to close this age out and open the new eternal one according to Revelation 5. Verses 9-10 call him worthy on three accounts:

He was willing to be slaughtered—he died for justice.

He purchased from every tribe, language, people—he is not racist or partial.

He established the redeemed ones as a heaven-to-earth connected kingdom—he brought in a new creation, a just world order.

Reflective Actions

Prayer | "Jesus, you alone are worthy to judge and wise enough to exact loving and redemptive revenge. How this works, I do not know. I need a fresh revelation of your nature! I open my heart to your goodness today."

Ask Your Father | "Do I really believe deep down that you are wise enough and good enough to set things back in order even though I still see pain, suffering and injustice now?" How else do you see enemies, Papa God? What is your heart for them?

Meditation | Do you see God as too good or too soft in that he may not exact a strong enough price for injustice? Or... do you see God as so angry with wickedness that you are scared of him? How good is God's goodness to you? Is it trustworthy in justice? Take some time to journal about this today.

Breakthrough | "Jesus, you ARE good and wise and holy and just! I trust you with all the rivers of my heart. I enter your kindness that leads to repentance, extending grace. For as I do, it will be done to me. Amen!"

[22] Letter 14 extra coll. (63).84

[23] Incomplete Work on Matthew, Homily 13

day 17

OVERCOME EVIL WITH GOOD

"Do not be overcome by evil, but overcome evil with good."

Romans 12:21, ESV Translation

The first part of the command, "do not be overcome" is a challenge to stand our ground, to endure the attack. Many of us feel we can go this far, though sometimes, when in the face of a continuous grinding evil, we begin to feel smoke-damaged by overexposure.

It is the second part of the command, "overcome evil with good" that really strikes fear in us. Is good really that powerful? I mean, will it be powerful enough for me in the face of my very real enemies? *The people of God are actually meant to proactively overcome evil with good, not only endure it but overcome it.*

Overcome is a command designed to bless us. The experience of walking this out will teach us we operate from a supernatural kingdom. Can we see ourselves as part of the new kingdom order bringing kind justice into this broken world? You might wonder: can my small handful of good overcome the powerful and evil people I'm facing? Maybe today evidence of breakthrough is invisible to the eye, but love in action will bring kingdom witness and create a place where light from heaven floods into dark places, scattering demons and setting principalities in their place. It will wreak havoc in the true enemies' camp.

How do we approach evil people with good? It begins with praying for them and using small acts of kindness. Michal Ann Goll, a compassion-motivated church leader, used to speak of a revolution of a movement of kindness. These words are worth frequent reflection. "What if the community of God was known for being outrageously kind? How much good would that create in our world today?"

Avoid reacting to evil defensively by making a case for yourself but respond offensively by making a case in kindness and love which you are 100% "in the right" to show.

Reflective Actions

Prayer | "Jesus, I want to overcome evil with radical kindness! Teach me to be proactive rather than reactive. I am an overcomer because of you and your goodness in my life!"

Ask Your Father | "What are small ways I can show kindness to my enemies?"

Meditation | Have fun and document the testimonies as a record of God's kindness and faithfulness!

Breakthrough | You don't need to act extra spiritual; simply give an act of kindness they can understand:

- » Send a small note, card or token gift. Bless their child. Visit them if they are sick and pray for them.

- » Give a generous love offering to some rebel leader, some refugees, a different church than yours, a Muslim family, a political leader in a different party, a competitor. Demonstrate love to them in a radical way.

- » Choose smart ways to disperse a larger gift directly like school supplies, medical assistance, or food.

- » Dig in today. Research a need. There is added strength in responding as a community or family.

day 18

ENEMIES ARE TREASURE

"For I am the least of the apostles, unworthy to be called an apostle, because I persecuted the church of God. But by the grace of God I am what I am, and his grace toward me was not in vain."

1 Corinthians 15:9-10, ESV Translation

These are personal words of Paul. He was an enemy of the Jerusalem church. He treated the church like "waste water"[24] (Acts 8:3). He did much evil to the Jerusalem saints (Acts 9:13). He persecuted the church excessively and tried to destroy it (Galatians 1:13).

From Paul's own experience of persecution by the Jewish religious community later, we can assume his harsh intentions against the church were expressed in legal trials, imprisonment, floggings, beatings, and even stoning people to death. He was not a nice guy. He was a violent religious extremist.

Imagine being in the Jerusalem church, and Paul walks in. Your friend nudges you in the ribs. Isn't that Saul, who they now call Paul? You glance at your aunt. She's pale, looking at the floor and biting her lower lip. *Did she recognize Paul?* You wonder. Her husband still has back pain, from the thrashing he got from Paul's religious thugs. Thoughts rip across your synapses, *Dad's cousin died in prison didn't he? That was from Paul too.* You hear muffled gasps, murmurs and see furtive glances Paul's direction.

Paul visiting the Jerusalem church was like a mass murderer who had destroyed almost half the people you loved and knew walking into the room. Was that easy for the early church? Don't you think many—maybe almost all—of them had some experience of injustice they had to swallow to accept Paul as a brother?

What if we never forgave and accepted Apostle Paul for the ways he persecuted Christians before his salvation? He might have never led thousands to know and experience Christ. We may not have any of Paul's incredibly inspired letters.

When the church forgave Paul, it led to a greater blessing than they could have imagined: their own enemy became their greatest asset. He wrote much of what is now our New Testament, and from what we understand, he was instrumental in expanding much of the early church outside of the Jewish community.

Reflective Actions

Prayer | "God, change my heart for my enemies..."

Ask Your Father | "Who is the Saul in my life? Show me how he/she becomes Paul?"

Meditation | Turn to Isaiah 58:9b-10. Meditate on how you speak. About how enemies may be afflicted and hungry for God. How our decisions about this impact our own spiritual atmosphere.

Breakthrough | "I speak a Damascus road encounter over them today! Saul will become Paul!" Write out who your enemy really is, their destiny to become another Paul. Fast at least one day requesting a heart that can see the treasure in those that are the very worst. Pray your "Saul to Paul" declarations over your enemy daily!

---

[24] See Greek usage of Paul laying waste.

"...quiet your soul and let his love satisfy you now."

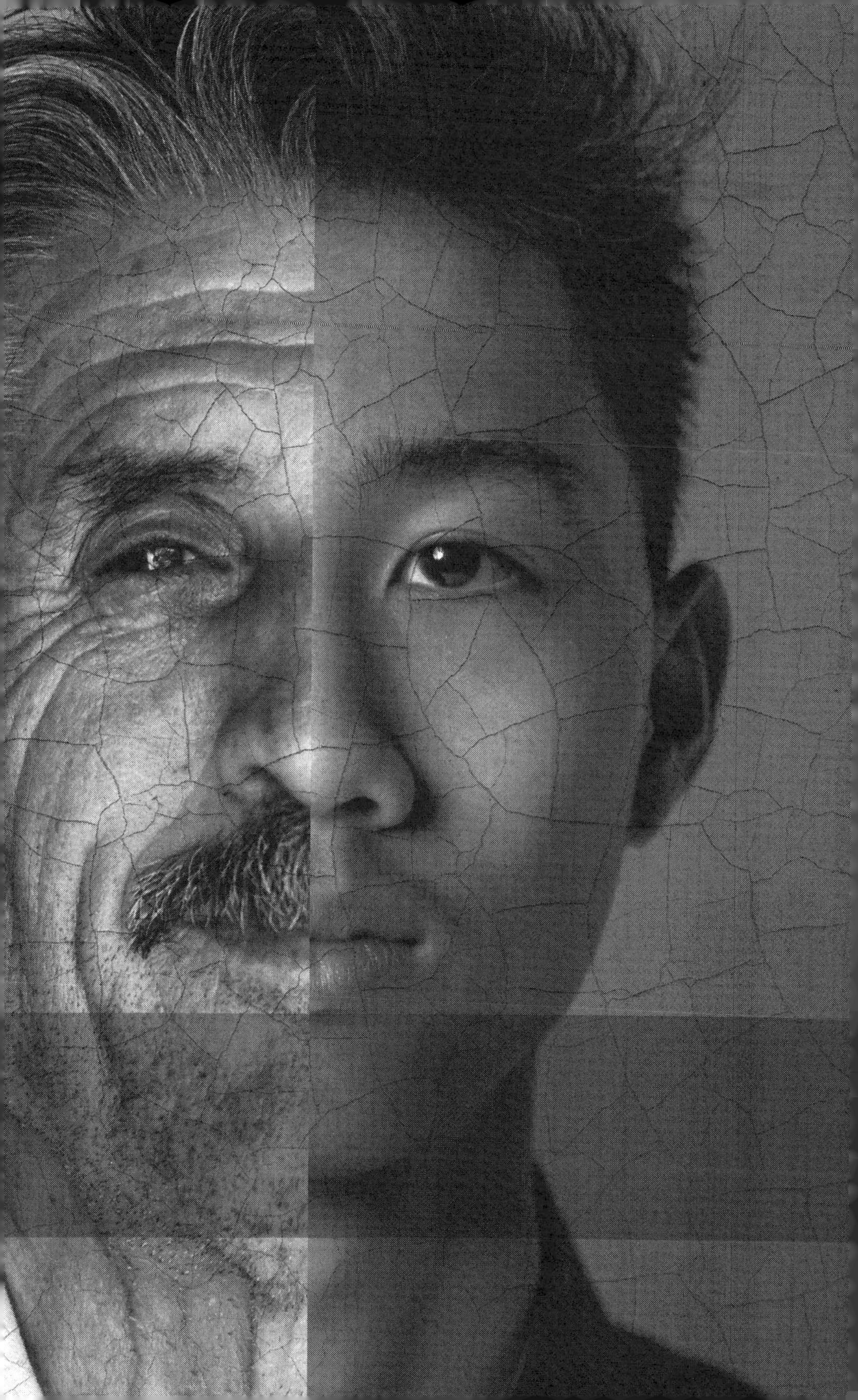

day 19 — HOW AN ENEMY BECOMES TREASURE

"But love your enemies, and do good, and lend, expecting nothing in return, and your reward will be great, and you will be sons of the Most High, for he is kind to the ungrateful and evil"
Luke 6:35, ESV Translation

Let's examine our perceptions about rewards. Is loving an enemy such a difficult task that God will acknowledge our amazing accomplishments before all of heaven and give us a hero's crown, heavy with jewels? After all, if Jesus said, giving a cup of cold water in his name would be rewarded,[25] how much more reward should there be for accepting a cup of betrayal for God's sake, like Jesus did on his journey of the cross to forgive us?[26] But could the reward Matthew and Luke speak about of loving enemies be something more life giving than an inanimate crown or even heavenly titles?

» What if... just knowing that I played a huge part in helping my enemies in their journey to redemption and usefulness to God is sweetness to my soul?

» What if... the pain my enemy caused increased the grace, joy and presence of Holy Spirit in my life?

» What if... my reward for loving an enemy is that they become an eternal and grateful friend?

» What if... my reward is discovering that my enemies are some of the costly treasures of Jesus' passion?

» What if... some of my enemies are designed by God to be the greatest leaders in his church in his redemptive character and plan?

The heart of the matter: Instead of seeking crowns in heaven and praise, let's just seek the beauty of one day standing hand in hand as brothers and sisters in Christ with our enemies, only now they are our eternal friends.

Empathy is the ability to stand in someone else's shoes and see life through their eyes. It is an elite form of humility and critical to peacemaking. Most people's anger and reactions are built on layers of choices that often trace back into childhood. When they treat you wrong, it is often not even you they are reacting to until you begin to react back towards them.

Reflective Actions

Prayer | "Lord Jesus, I pray healing for my enemies' wounds; bring the balm of your kindness and mercy to them in their pain. Help me to step into their shoes and give me your strategies of determined love to help them."

Ask Your Father | "What childhood wounds are my enemies' actions rooted in?" Look at family, local culture, and history. "Father, how do you desire to heal the wounds of their heart?"

Meditation | Look at the list of rewards above. Which one attracts you most and why? Whichever one that is, take some time to pray into it and choose a specific action you can do today.

Breakthrough | "Father, your desire is to heal my enemy and to use me to partner in this healing! I accept the challenge. Show me how I can proactively bring healing to them today!" For example, want an enemy to become a godly leader? Write a social media post about their potential! How powerful, both for your own heart and for turning others' eyes to see what is possible in God!

---

[25] Matthew 10:42

[26] Luke 22:42

day 20
THE MINISTRY OF RECONCILIATION

"But Ananias answered, 'Lord, I have heard from many about this man, how much evil he has done to your saints at Jerusalem. And here he has authority from the chief priests to bind all who call on your name.' But the Lord said to him, 'Go, for he is a chosen instrument of mine to carry my name...'"

Acts 9:13-15a, ESV Translation

When God asked Ananias to go to Paul, Ananias was like, "Are you sure, God?!"

There is a story of a young man who was a former Muslim and assassin. He had completed over 26 political assassinations before he met Jesus. His friends would internally react when he shared his story. He recounted how he gloated for months after he had shot his first "Christian" 40 times when he was just 14 years old and other terrible scenes of death. Friends would think, 'This man is a killer. Shouldn't he be in prison?' But instead, here he was, their friend! He was serving children at risk in Muslim communities where much conflict was present. Is this possibly just a little bit of what it was like for the early church to accept Paul, her chief "enemy" standing before them in the flesh?

"So Ananias departed and entered the house. And laying his hands on him he said, 'Brother Saul, the Lord Jesus who appeared to you on the road by which you came has sent me so that you may regain your sight and be filled with the Holy Spirit.' And immediately something like scales fell from his eyes, and he regained his sight (Acts 9:17-18, ESV).

If we are not willing to personally bring the words of deliverance to our enemies, even if they have a face-to-face encounter with Jesus, it may not be enough. This is because God holds me responsible to carry the words of reconciliation that can take the demonic blinders of hatred from my enemies' eyes. We are commissioned as God's reconcilers to bring the Holy Spirit to God's enemies and our enemies.

Reflective Actions

Prayer | "Jesus, I long to give you an emphatic 'yes' in every area of my life. And I say 'yes' now in faith to the call to bring deliverance to my enemies. Help this to resonate with faith in my heart as I speak it."

Ask Your Father | "Is God calling me to be an Ananias? To reconcile one of the worst of these as a living statement of who my Papa really is? Who are you sending me to?"

Meditation | Truth: I can heal the blind eyes of my enemy as a powerful ambassador of your kingdom on earth.

Breakthrough | It's God's pleasure to make sure you have plenty of ambassadorial opportunities to reconcile with people, demonstrating the heart of Jesus' gospel. Find someone in your community to reconcile with. Anyone.

See if your church can "adopt" a rebel leader, mafia boss, disliked politician or a church leader fallen from grace in your community. Craft a letter of blessing from the church to this person. Have a church leader or elder offer to host them for a nice meal. Do you have any skilled people in your congregation that could serve them with something? A free dental checkup? Cleaning their car? What acts of service can you offer?

LAUGH AT THE CHALLENGE

day 21

> *"He who sits in the heavens laughs; the Lord holds them in derision. Then he will speak to them in his wrath, and terrify them in his fury, saying, 'As for me, I have set my King on Zion, my holy hill.'"*
>
> **Psalm 2:4-6, ESV Translation**

Do I believe our God is big enough for the problem of enemies? Is His love strong enough to suffer for them? Is His death on a cross potent enough to go low to rescue them? Is His love tough enough to win them? Is His resurrection glorious enough to sweep them up into a loving Father's arms?

Psalm 2 speaks of Jesus. Acts 4 verifies this messianic vibrance for us when the early church prays Psalm 2 when Peter and John returned safe from prison. The Psalm speaks of all the people and their rulers plotting against Jesus. How he laughs at them, joyful in the rage of his enemies. The Aramaic translation "the Lord holds them in derision" replaces Lord with Logos,[27] "the Word holds them in derision."

Jesus, the unstoppable, prophetic Word of the Father, broke into the earthly realm to receive the full wrath of God. It was a terrifying moment. Thick darkness swallowed the land. The temple curtain tore with an earthquake. Rocks cracked like eggs, graves yawned open, hungry for the resurrection. On that day of wrath, Jesus was set on a cross as "King of the Jews" on the holy hill of Zion, a redemptive crown of thorns bleeding across his brow for a world of enemies.

And as this happened God laughed, "You are all so clueless! You still can't imagine the vast goodness of my heart, but I'm showing it to you now in my cross and resurrection!" At the resurrection many dead people were restored to life and wandered into Jerusalem—good news!

So why am I still limiting God by thinking this enemy needs to immediately find a permanent labor camp in hell? Maybe I don't want my enemy to say yes to Jesus.

Maybe I can't endure this enemy any longer.

If you are still struggling with loving an enemy, know that this is a moment you were made for. God dearly wants you to experience the lavish riches of his grace through your journey of loving enemies, to laugh with kind gladness at enemies!

Reflective Actions

Prayer | "Jesus, let your joy seep into every area of my heart and life!"

Ask Your Father | "Please show me any part of my heart that doesn't want my enemy to know Jesus' love and joy."

Meditation | Take a break. Walk in a park. Let gladness fill your soul. Go outside, away from city lights, and gaze into the dark cosmos and glassy stars. Watch a sunrise and allow its beauty to stretch your soul wide. Know that God is so much bigger than any enemy problem. Hold this joy and let it be your battle weapon.

Breakthrough | "I was made for this crazy ministry of reconciliation under a cross more powerful than any enemy! I reject anger and hatred and step into joy. I laugh joyfully at the plans of the real spiritual enemy against me and also (name your enemy). Hahaha!"

---

[27] Memra (Aram. אֲרָמִימ 'word') see The Oxford Dictionary of the Christian Church (3rd ed. rev., p. 1076). Oxford; New York: Oxford University Press.

day 22
WAS JESUS EVER MEAN?

"And making a whip of cords, he drove them all out of the temple, with the sheep and oxen. And he poured out the coins of the money-changers and overturned their tables."

John 2:15, ESV Translation

What is Jesus' real-life example for me in loving enemies? Didn't he curse a fig tree, cuss out Pharisees and scribes, and take a whip to the temple vendors? Why should I bless all the time, speak kindly to stuck up hypocrites who hate me and not defend my property like Jesus defended his temple?

Don't box a perfect Jesus into our world as his personal restrictions are, um... godlike. This is not to take God off the hook for rudeness, but he can do things in love and wisdom that we can never get away with.

Jesus commanded the fig tree to cease life because it followed the curse of not bearing in every season. He was prophetically speaking of a new age, where his people would have faith to be ever-bearing fruit, and he was looking towards his soon-cleansing of the temple. Jesus was on earth to institute a new world order, the current sacrificial system was superficial, and Jesus, the anointed king, was the only sacrifice for the entire world forever and ever amen. Looking at the broken Passover system was highly distressing to him. Someone so much better was present and people were blind to HIM who is the Redeemer in their temple.

Scriptures never say Jesus struck anyone, that is our quick assumption. He drove out the sheep and oxen, paused the sale of doves. He stopped the sacrificial system because he was the sacrificial Lamb of God. After he cleared the temple grounds he demonstrated his true heart. The blind and the lame came to him there and he healed them. Little children ran around the courtyard playing and singing, "Hosanna to the Son of David!" (See The Gospel of Matthew's version of the story, chapter 12.)

Jesus sees a human heart from every dimension. But even if we have a revelation, a word from heaven, or are simply really wise and discerning regarding someone's heart, we still "see through a glass darkly."[28] *Don't think for a moment you know someone's heart, especially an enemy's heart, well enough to judge it. Tread the sacred ground of speaking judgment cautiously.*

Jesus was not focused on being nice but on helping people find an abundance of living waters—Life. Jesus at times ferociously verbally barraged religious leaders who blockaded truth. He rarely confronted everyday people, but he made an exception for religious shepherds keeping his cherished flock from Life.

Reflective Actions

Prayer | "Jesus, I want to be a life giver like you, whether I am angry, sad or just feeling like me."

Ask Your Father | Worshipfully seek God's presence. Ask, "Father, how do you love me?" Treasure what he says.

Meditation | Journal these questions: When someone meets you, can they have a spiritual moment? Can an enemy look you in the eye and see Jesus' love? Do you impart hope or leak negativity? Can you rebuke an enemy and still show Jesus' true heart? Is the presence of God reflected in what you do and say?

Breakthrough | Remember that moment you sat in God's love? Now you have a snapshot for the way your enemy needs to hear from you. I am outrageously loved, and therefore I carry outrageous love!

---

[28] 1 Corinthians 13:12

day 23

DON'T FEAR YOUR ENEMY

"Behold, I am sending you out as sheep in the midst of wolves, so be wise as serpents and innocent as doves."

Matthew 10:16, ESV Translation

Do not fear, perfect little lamb, I'm sending you into a pack of wolves. You are the life giver; they are the life takers. I am in you: the very Life source that the wolves need. If you survive, it will be a miracle. You believe in my many, many miracles, do you not?

Little sheep, don't be foolish. Remember that serpent who fooled Eve into thinking she needed something more. You are perfect because I have called you a lamb. You were chosen to feed wolves. They do bite, but they don't understand the power of the Life that is in you. Use your weapons well. They think you are only a lamb, but you are far more. You are carrying their only hope. Ten thousand angels stand ready to assist you on your journey. Don't be anxious, child. If you begin to feel soiled by the wolf pack, remember the dove. Take her wings of morning hope, soar high with me for a while in prayer and worship. I am pure love.

These Matthew 10:16 words of Jesus were spoken at a time when he was sending his disciples out two by two. First, he sent out the twelve disciples, and then the seventy-two.

Isn't it interesting that Jesus sent his key leaders like sheep into the midst of wolves? When we picture sheep and wolves, it usually involves the enemy wolves dominating the terrified sheep. Jesus' picture is radically different. It is a paradoxical image of God's love softly conquering evil through us.

We are called to be wooly sheep running in the snarling wolf pack. In practicality, this means the best place to build Jesus' church is in the midst of enemies—growing communities of life in dark places while living the good news.

How can harmless lambs be a danger to wolves? Could God's love be more dangerous than an enemy wolf's bite? Do we dare live this in real life? The answer is: yes.

Reflective Actions

Prayer | "I so want to believe in your tender goodness as you send me, a sheep, out to the wolves. Help me, Jesus!"

Ask Your Father | "Do you really love me, Papa? If you love me, then why send me to the wolves?"

Meditation | "For I tell you, unless your righteousness exceeds that of the scribes and Pharisees, you will never enter the kingdom of heaven" (Matthew 5:20, ESV). Our experience of Jesus' love puts us on a higher plane than duty. There is something radically beyond religion when a sheep follows the Shepherd into the midst of wolves.

Breakthrough | "It is not about who I can be, but instead who I already am and who YOU are inside of me! You have made me new through your son! I choose my new creation purpose instead of choosing the old life, a decaying corpse. I choose to be who you already made me to be."

"If you love me, then why send me to the wolves?"

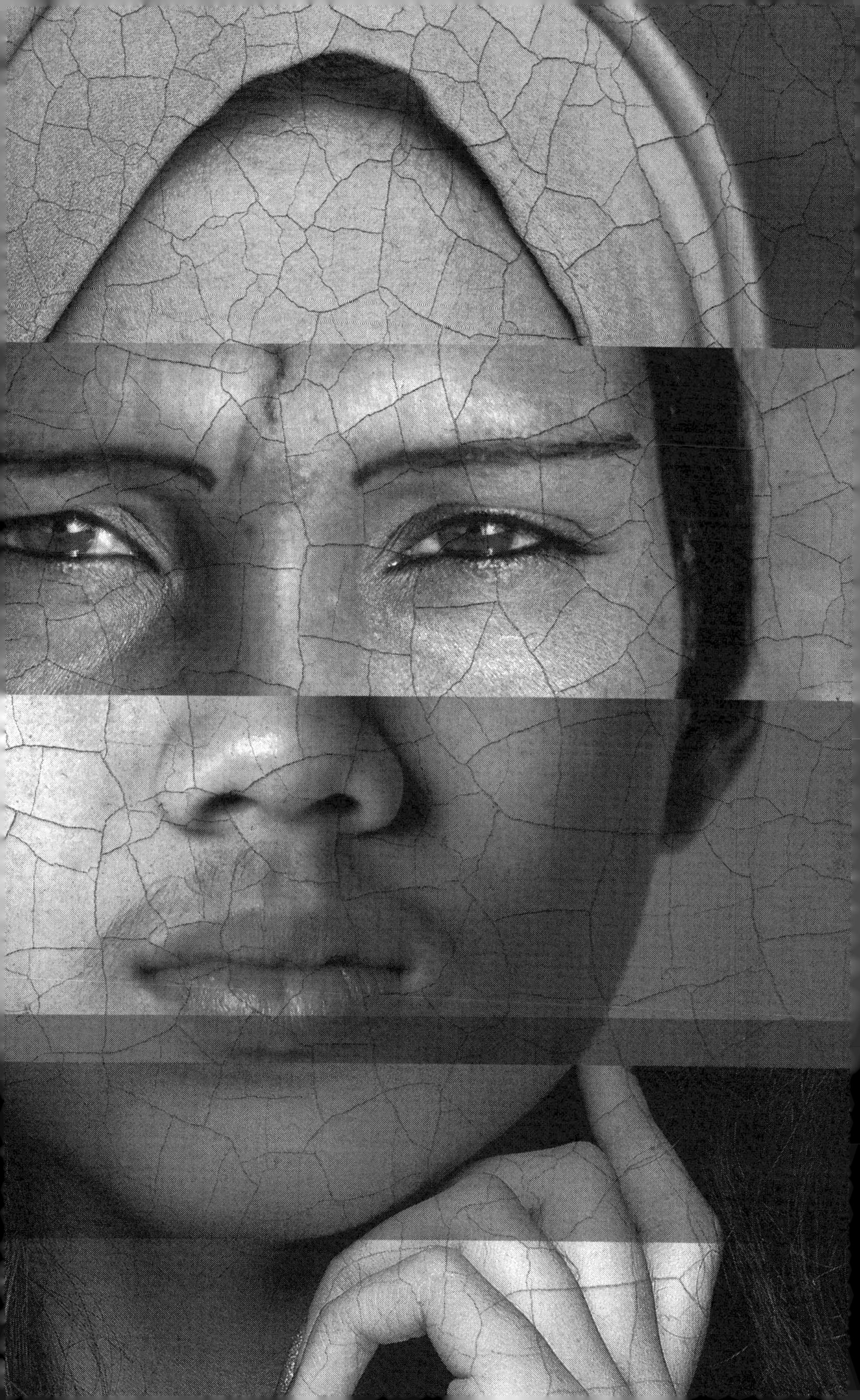

day 24
PERFECT FOR ENEMIES

"You therefore must be perfect, as your heavenly Father is perfect."

Matthew 5:48, ESV Translation

This is Jesus' capstone statement about loving enemies from Matthew 5:43-48: "be perfect like your heavenly Father." Your heavenly Father loves enemies, and he considers loving enemies a measure of perfection. This is the measuring stick for all the Christian perfectionists out there. It is not easy though. Loving enemies is messy. Rarely does loving look or feel perfect.

Maybe we are at a good point to pause and remember that *loving an enemy is a journey that perfects us in love and proves our family ties with heaven, which ultimately brings us great joy and peace.*

Luke's 6:36 rendition reads: "Be merciful just as your Father is merciful!" Mercy is what we give enemies, and we reflect the perfect One when we give this mercy. In the Scriptures the word for "perfect" is sometimes translated as "mature," while the Aramaic word Jesus may have used when actually teaching this carries nuances of wholeness.

Loving enemies is the best way we can create a perfect picture of who the Father is for the world he created. We could call this perfect kind of love one of Jesus' powerful strategies for societal transformation. But it is not a natural kind of love. If we were to live out loving enemies "naturally," it would eventually only create more wars. Either we would choose selfish ways to show love that created offense, or we would follow the "rules" of loving enemies and miss the heart of it. Enemy-focused love is perfection from heaven, it is God's big, "I forgive you, and I love you," to everyone in the world through Jesus. In us, it is a divine encounter of love overflowing to others.

Reflective Actions

Prayer | "Holy Spirit, I invite a divine encounter of your love today as I work, pray, break bread, and sleep. Speak to my heart and rekindle your love. My Father, let your vast love for me, your son/daughter, become a flame of love for all the enemies of the world: those I dislike, those that anger me, those the world hates."

Ask Your Father | "As a follower of Jesus, who do I still fear? The intellectual atheist? Fellowship with a democrat, socialist or republican? Those of other ethnicities or skin tones? The urban poor or eccentric rich? A parent or child? A homosexual or religious bigot? A terrorist or a human trafficker? A prostitute or child soldier?"

Meditation | The kingdom of Love is bold. "There is no fear in love, but perfect love casts out fear. For fear has to do with punishment, and whoever fears has not been perfected in love. We love because he first loved us" (1 John 4:18-19, ESV). Meditate here and allow Holy Spirit to work on his masterpiece of you, a true picture of Papa God's heart by loving your enemies. What better gift can we offer the world than this?

Breakthrough | "Jesus, I am a beautiful reflection of you to your cosmos, to the powers and principalities, to the rulers and to the small and the forgotten! I give you my little yes. And I know you will make it a massive YES so that others see you and glorify you, Papa!"

day 25

HONOR YOUR ENEMIES
PART 1

"The Lord forbid that I should do this thing to my lord, the Lord's anointed, to put out my hand against him, seeing he is the Lord's anointed."

1 Samuel 24:6, ESV Translation

David and his men crept further back into in the darkest shadows of the cave as the soldiers milled around the bright entrance, some peering in. Then to David's surprise, King Saul, his chief nemesis, stepped into the dim light of the cave's mouth. Saul meandered into the shadows and squatted down, pulled his cloak aside and began to relieve himself.

David hissed, "Men, stay here!" Acting decisively as military men do, he crept near Saul, then quietly sawed the corner of his robe off. Seconds afterwards, his conscience stabbed him. Even in this small act of defiance towards this demonized yet still anointed king, David's greatest enemy, he realized deep in his heart that he was moving away from alignment with God's kingdom.

One of the best ways to strengthen a pure heart is by showing honor. David had an easy opportunity to kill Saul, who was out to murder him. By refusing to do this in spite of peer pressure, he passed a critical test. David's test of his growing leadership was giving honor, even for his evil leaders. This was his path to true governance—political power aligned to heaven. "Honor all people. Love the brotherhood. Fear God. Honor the king" (1 Peter 2:17, NKJV).

Our ability to see God directly correlates with the purity of our hearts: to be like Jesus, seeing what the Father is doing and aligning our activity to him. Without a pure heart, I offer only hollow honor for others. Pure honor is potent honor. *Pure honor can realign an enemy's activities to heaven's as in Saul's case when David shared his heart with Saul when they met again outside the cave.*

David followed Saul out. Bowing down in honor, he called out, "Some told me to kill you, but I spared you, see the corner of your robe in my hand!" When David finished speaking, Saul asked, "Is this your voice, my son David?" And Saul lifted up his voice and wept. Then he said to David, "You are more righteous than I, for you have repaid me good, whereas I have repaid you evil" (1 Samuel 24:8-17).

Reflective Actions

Prayer | "Father, I want to honor you by honoring enemies. I want them to see YOU when they look at me."

Ask Your Father | "Do I have the purity of heart or hunger to see you at work in my enemy's heart? Is there anything I have observed in my life, my church and community that triggers me to dishonor your enemies?"

Meditation | Read back over 1 Samuel 24:8-17. Notice Saul shifts from seeing David as an enemy to a son because of the honor David gives him as a leader. How can I be a son/daughter or father/mother to my enemy?

Breakthrough | I am already pure because of God's Word. I am his beloved child. I can rest in the power of a child's love and innocence with my enemies. It is God who has put this grace of a child into me. Child is what he calls me. It is how he holds me in the heart of my persecution, his kind arms wrapped around me.

day 26

HONOR YOUR ENEMIES
PART 2

"Belteshazzar answered and said, 'My lord, may the dream be for those who hate you and its interpretation for your enemies!'"

Daniel 4:19, ESV Translation

Daniel, or Belteshazzar by his Babylonian name, was scared and the king knew it. "Speak it out, Daniel!" King Nebuchadnezzar ordered. He was not a nice guy on a daily basis. He had recently tried to kill Daniel's three dear friends—Shadrach, Meshach and Abednego—for not bowing down to his image. He had also carried them all from their homeland as teenagers after besieging their beloved Jerusalem. Later, he dismantled Solomon's temple. This desecration was unthinkable.

Daniel stood under the intense gaze of this powerful and proud man, an enemy of his people. He had just heard the dream that was troubling Nebuchadnezzar. He knew very clearly what it meant, there was no doubt on this. But how would Nebuchadnezzar view the message from heaven?

Taking a deep breath, Daniel began with a formality common in his day,[29] "May this happen to your enemies instead!" He really wasn't wishing judgment on anyone, he was simply formally honoring the king. Perhaps some warmth had developed between Nebuchadnezzar and Daniel over time but the critical point is: Daniel knew how to honor an enemy.

After finishing the interpretation—a stern sentence from angels—Daniel wasn't done. He still cared enough to give Nebuchadnezzar a path out of coming judgment. "Here is my counsel O King, break off your sins by practicing what is right, give mercy to the poor, and maybe God will extend your reign."[30]

Daniel didn't try to steer the wicked king into judgment, he instead attempted to steer him into repentance so that he wouldn't be judged. The heart of honor is this: *it keeps someone else's best interests in mind.*

Because Daniel wisely counseled the king, even though it took many years, Nebuchadnezzar came to his senses and reigned in humility before his death. In context of the story, the poor received mercy during his latter reign. *How you treat an enemy, doesn't simply impact them, it also impacts their circle of influence.*

Reflective Actions

Prayer | "Teach me to honor my enemies not simply for their sake alone, but also for those under their influence."

Ask Your Father | "Am I hurting or helping your kingdom plan by how I think, talk or act regarding my enemy?"

Meditation | Consider your enemy prayerfully: How do you feel God might want to use your enemy to demonstrate his kind mercy to those who desperately need it; their family, friends or others they influence?

Breakthrough | "Nebuchadnezzar was so full of himself that he built a great statue of his own likeness and commanded the entire kingdom to worship it. God, considering your heart for the king shown through Daniel, how much more do you desire the same change in the heart of my enemy? I lay down every thought and mindset that would contradict this heart of honor and love so that I can be your partner in influencing the world."

---

[29] See 1 Samuel 25.26 and 2 Samuel 18.32 for further examples

[30] Translation by Marcus Young

day 27 — CHASE YOUR ENEMIES
PART 1

"You shall chase your enemies, and they shall fall before you by the sword. Five of you shall chase a hundred, and a hundred of you shall chase ten thousand, and your enemies shall fall before you by the sword."

Leviticus 26:7-8, ESV Translation

This passage unlocks the glorious future of God's people when they love their enemies. Although this passage was written to Old Testament Israel, there is a New Testament lens through Jesus. His words in Matthew 5 about loving enemies still apply today:

You will chase your enemies with the life-giving words of Jesus' love and grace, and they will fall before you. Even five of you joining together will route a small army. If one thousand of you paint big targets of Heaven's love on your enemies and pursue them, then the fame of God's possession, his church, will accelerate globally.

This process begins small. It starts with a few scattered people acting counter-culturally, showing love to someone who does not merit it. When many thousands of people make a pattern of loving enemies, it becomes a revolution. Would you be part of a Love Your Enemy Movement?

As we near the end of our 30-day quest together, imagine a church that has a reputation in every community of truly loving enemies. Imagine they have a reputation of blessing instead of judging, of honoring enemies with kindness and fighting for their best, of only confronting enemies when they deeply care for them. Imagine a reputation of loving them with the crazy love God showed by sending his very best, his beloved Son, into the fire ants' nest of enemies on planet earth.

Could the good news of Jesus explode with this kind of love shown by me?

Reflective Actions

Prayer | "Jesus, please strengthen me to be an intentional lover of enemies. I'm not talking about a mushy thing. I want your titanium backbone of not backing down. I know I can't do everything, so I ask you to show me 'crazy love' things I can do to demonstrate your heart."

Ask Your Father | "How did you pursue me to win me? How are you pursuing my enemy today?"

Meditation | Does it ever bother you that people struggle to see the heart of God behind the story of our gospel? Would you be willing to make steps towards radically loving enemies to change this? How can you light fires for loving enemies where you are? How can you do this in your workplace or your school?

Breakthrough | "Jesus, you have given me courage and passion for this mission! Now give me divine moments of opportunity and creative inspiration for extravagant expression of your kindness! Give me joy that sparkles when I face my enemies!"

day 28 — CHASE YOUR ENEMIES
PART 2

"In the same way, let your light shine before others, that they may see your good deeds and glorify your Father in heaven."

Matthew 5:16, New International Version

God has called us to pursue our enemies in love. So, who is an enemy you can pursue? It is good to begin to target the people we feel are the least worthy and most evil in our world and make it a goal to overwhelm them with love. But some of those people are far from us. How do we exemplify love to the enemies not only close to home but also far away?

Light is very noticeable in a dark place. We can think about loving enemies such as ISIS leaders, traffickers, extortionists, dark net hackers or gangsters. These are wonderful love targets! But what about that lawsuit we are in, our ex-spouse, the beloved-in-heaven immigrants or slum dwellers a few neighborhoods across the way? The people who taint our politics and make us shudder? These describe just a few of those we should target with divine love.

How can we live Love Your Enemy globally as we watch countries go to war and tyrannical leaders sabotage local economics? And how can we live this locally at the coffee shop and grocery store? Those we consider enemies should experience the love of Jesus' church through aggressive kindness. Do they? *We should be famous for loving our enemies, especially the most evil, unimaginably awful in our world.*

We have reached a climax in our Loving Enemies journey: committing to pray for and love our enemies in such a radical way that the world pays attention.

In the early church of Acts 2, Christians were both feared and respected by those on the outside. Our enemies should both fear and have a healthy respect for the power of our love assailing their hearts. This intensity of expressing the heart of heaven is a strategic reason why Jesus told us to love our enemies. *It has demonstrative power to shift people's understanding of the church and the God she reflects.*

Our love becomes a revolution that wins lost children of the world over to their good Father. We have reached the place in our journey where it is time to make a massive statement to our enemies:

Reflective Actions

Prayer | "Make my love an enemy revolution: 'Our love is loud, our love is strong, our love is for you because of Jesus Christ!'"

Ask Your Father | "How can my community and I go the extra mile to make a HUGE impact? What can we do that would shock the world with our love?"

Meditation | As you search your heart, ponder and listen to Holy Spirit and jot down specific ways to put this to action. Don't discount small steps forward. Small steps forward are powerful and create momentum in our lives.

Breakthrough | "Jesus, I choose today to leave the 99 and run with you after the 1! I AM READY! I was made for this kind of radical love revolution!"

"Our love is loud, our love is strong, our love is for you because of Jesus Christ!"

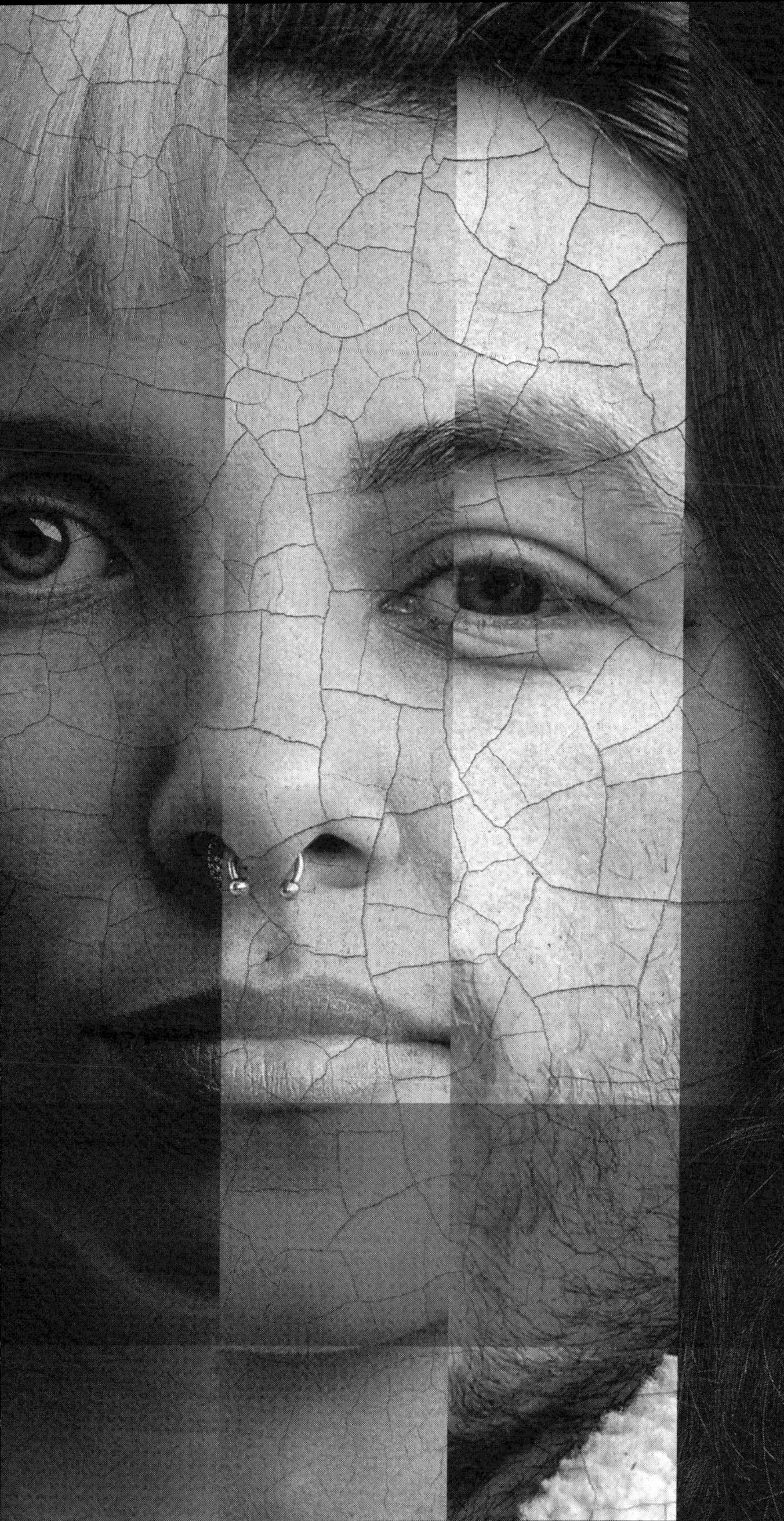

day 29
CELEBRATE GOD WITH YOUR ENEMIES

"Even though I walk through the valley of the shadow of death, I will fear no evil, for you are with me; your rod and your staff, they comfort me. You prepare a table before me in the presence of my enemies."

Psalm 23:4-5, ESV Translation

No need to be anxious about sudden evil from my enemy; even in dangerous places, my comforting Guide is always close. God even plans celebration feasts for me in the middle of enemy territory!

There is a fantastic spread on this table. There are revelations of God's heart for me. If I am willing to go low in humility to hear from my enemy, there is a correlated escalation of God's voice to me. God's encouragement for us to walk as overcomers will increase just like in Gideon's story when God sent him into the enemy's camp to hear warriors' dreams of his own victory over them in war.

But the main course of the banquet is the freedom of forgiveness. Hold on here, this forgiveness of enemies is far more sumptuous than it may sound! In the presence of enemies, we either forgive or die a spiritual death. There is no compromise here, but this works in our favor...

Forgiveness leads to understanding. It unblocks the doorways of our soul. Think about a God who forgave the entire world and what kind of vast understanding must emanate from him by considering all the ways he has forgiven us. His loving heart is greatly magnified by his forgiveness.

God's Spirit is the freest Spirit in the universe because of his never-ending forgiveness. Every act of forgiveness sends the human spirit higher and freer to enjoy the heavenly places. True forgiveness requires an empathetic depth of humility, a willingness to apologize to someone that has gone lower in character than us.

It is the humble who, by listening well, discover the deep things, the wisdom ways of heaven. Though it may be difficult, God will be your gracious host in the presence of your enemies. Consider it a feast that may not be easy to take the first bites of, but as we eat, we acquire a rare and precious wisdom.

Reflective Actions

Prayer | "God, could you give me different eyes and ears for enemies so I hear you through people I don't even like?"

Ask Your Father | "Do you find in me an unreserved love for enemies with no strings attached? Show me again how you have loved me through every season of my reconciliation to you to make my heart free to love."

Meditation | Ponder this scripture and dig out the joy. "Blessed are you when people insult you and persecute you, and falsely say all kinds of evil against you because of me. Rejoice and be glad, for your reward in heaven is great; for in the same way they persecuted the prophets who were before you" (Matthew 5:11-12, NASB).

Breakthrough | "Thank you for your Father's heart over me as your child, that same fierce love you have for Jesus. It's so good! Thank you also for the great gift in loving enemies and the beautiful shaping you are doing in my life through them. Free my heart, Papa God. I want to soar free in a love like you have for your world."

day 30

FIND REST WITH YOUR ENEMIES

"The Lord says to my Lord: "Sit at my right hand, until I make your enemies your footstool."

Psalms 110:1, ESV Translation

Enemies are meant to be a resting place for our weary feet on the journey into abundant life.

In scripture, God's footstools are described in three ways – the earth[31], the temple[32], and his enemies. The earth is God's creation and it is good. He loves it. He rested in all his goodness after creation. The temple was a God-inspired creation of man. So God loved it. His glory even rested in this temple that men crafted for him. Enemies? When Jesus makes enemies a footstool, they become a resting place for nail-scarred feet. Yes, he loves enemies too.

Ultimately, any spiritual victory over enemies is the work of God. Beyond our obedience to love our enemies, God is the one who does rescuing and transformational beauty work in their hearts.

Often, the most powerful work we can do is rest our faith in a God who is great. God's desire for us to have rest (Sabbath) is evident all throughout scripture. In Isaiah 58 for example, we are taught that in the "true fast" God is looking for acts of justice and mercy, but the passage ends by advising us to love the Sabbath—which is rest.

In a similar pattern, take time to rest this day in God's completed work regarding our enemies. Besides, you have already joined the fight for kind justice this past month. Let God build his house and woo his enemies through your rest in him. Allow the act of the cross to do its work.

Reflective Actions

Prayer | "Holy Spirit, you come to my rescue in prayer. When I am tired, you can carry the day" (Romans 8:26-28).

Ask Your Father | "What are some of your thoughts you have about me and the ways my heart has aligned more with yours during this month of prayer and stepping out in love?"

Meditation | Journal the thoughts Papa had for you. Consider truths you've learned and review them daily this week. How has this journey of loving enemies redefined or refined your view of yourself? Find rest in any words Papa God has spoken.

Breakthrough | Receive the Father's vast pleasure over you for taking this journey of learning how to love enemies. Even if you didn't feel that you made much progress, quiet your soul and let his love satisfy you now. Our smallest steps towards love make his heart glad!

"Thank you, God, for your finished work on the cross that has already triumphed, even for my enemies. I have a beautiful love in you, Jesus, beyond understanding, vaster than creation. I rest my faith in the intense love that you have for me. It is a heavenly love, so powerful that nothing will ever stand in its way." Read Romans 8:38-39.

---

[31] Matthew 5:35

[32] 1 Chronicles 28:2

FINAL THOUGHTS

Were you convicted about expressing the potent love of God to your enemies as you read this? I was often, and I wrote this! Holy Spirit's conviction is a healthy experience, drawing us deeper into God's love and patient grace.

God will contend with his enemies as the church aligns with heaven in love and courage to pursue them in supernatural love. I hope that this 30-day journey has enlarged your heart and empowered you to represent the government of heaven.

May you boldly carry the loving good news of Jesus in your mediations, your conversations, and in the steps of your feet. You carry a message that is bright and beautiful, thoroughly irresistible and fearful to all of our enemies.

Maybe you have been so inspired by this 30-day journey that it stirs you to want to go to a dark place where enemies flourish like weeds.

Frontline workers often live under harsh conditions. They learn to thrive in isolated regions and harsh or violent cultures. They face various challenges—armed conflict, threats, persecution, exposure to disease and emotional stress in their continuous obedience to God's call of love. If your heart is flaming at these words, whether you are in preparation mode or go mode, run forward, go hard, hold strong in joy.

You can be a frontline lover of enemies right in the middle of everyday. It doesn't matter where you are, how small you feel, just walk under the banner of Love Your Enemies and we will make Jesus' name famous among the nations!

Want more?

Have a need to do something crazy for an enemy today?

Find a picture of an "enemy." Frame it and put it on your wall for target practice in prayer of mercy. Put it on your cellphone or your computer. Look at that person. See them through Jesus' eyes.

Do something crazy like print a t-shirt with the face of a terrorist or nasty politician on it along with a blessing structured on Philippians 4:8 (review Day 12). Become a radical person of faith and blessing for your enemies.

Share your best "love my enemy" ideas with us at LYE@IN-Fire.org

Join the Love Your Enemies Movement today! IN-Fire.org/LYE

GRATITUDE & ACKNOWLEDGEMENTS

My wife, Alyxius, who was one of the original editors and encouragers for this book.

My parents, Phil and Ruth, who have modeled overcoming evil with good.

The Just Projects Philippines team, who helped launch LYE on the ground in Mindanao.

Our CommunKniTies friends, and especially Joi Maniego-Iyorwa who help develop LYE 1.0 content into a 30-day field copy.

Lacie and Joel Hill for their edits coming from a deep passion for loving enemies, and especially Lacie for helping develop the Reflective Actions.

Brett Thompson for his amazing graphic design work.

Salutes to creatives like Travis Frugé and Wendell Moon. Gratitude to my daughter-in-law AJ Young and to AnneMarie McPherson, both fantastic editors and proofers.

And oh yes, all those wonderful and sometimes very challenging enemies who started me on this journey many years ago...

83

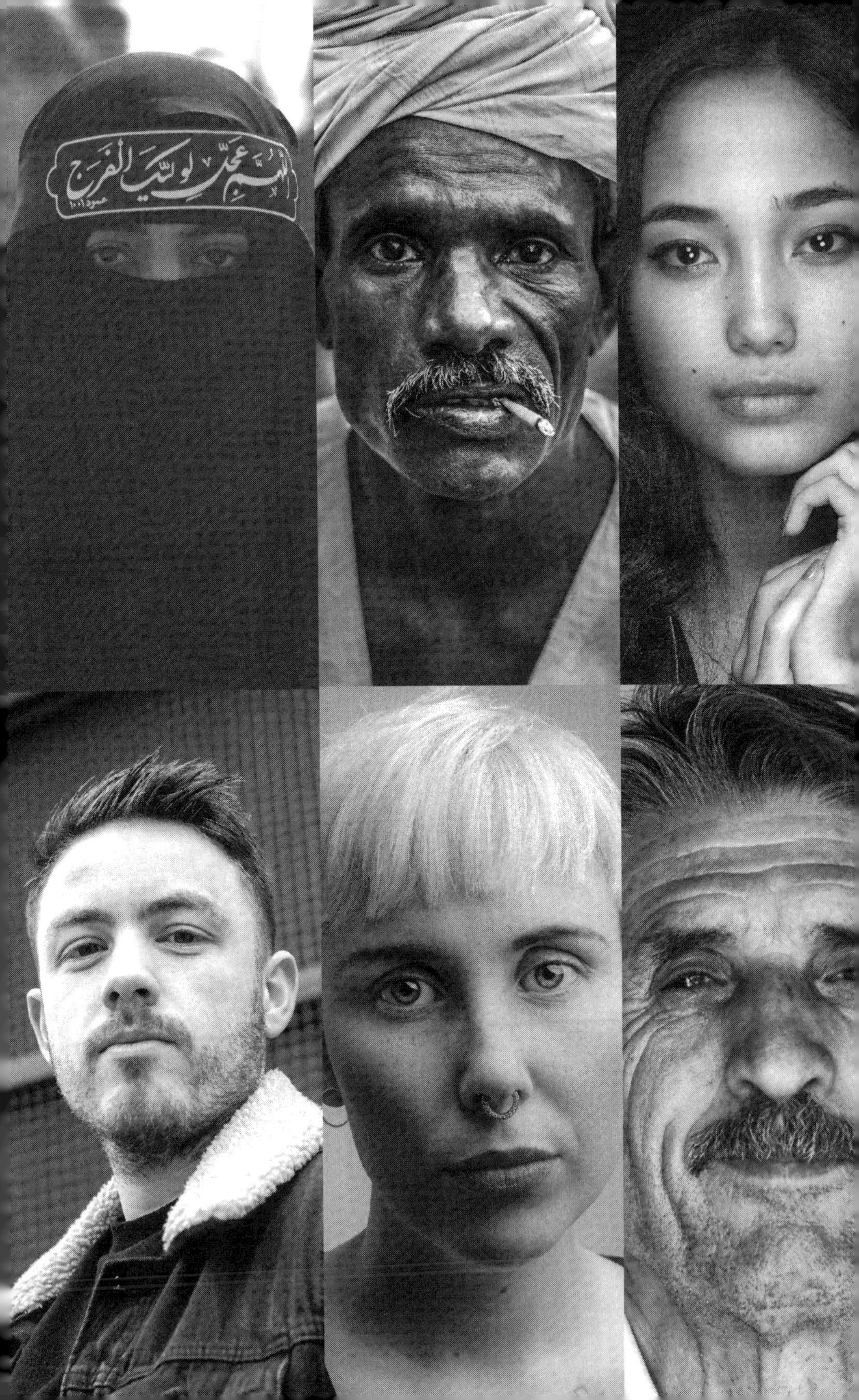
اللهم عجل لوليك الفرج

Printed in Great Britain
by Amazon